Kindergarten Readiness Brain Training Bundle

Bridgette Sharp

Table of Contents

Brain Training

Colors

red   black   purple   blue

red   black   purple

orange   white   blue

yellow   brown   green

green   brown   yellow

What is Brain Training?

Brain Training consists of many different programs designed to improve brain processing speed, hemispheric integration between the right and left brain, as well as internal brain timing and sequencing.

The exercises in this book are one method of hemispheric integration. While the right brain identifies the color, the left brain is utilized to read the shapes, numbers and words. As each exercise is done, the right and left brain must communicate to complete the task. This encourages the neurons to connect. Neurons that fire together wire together. Therefore, the more often the exercises are done, the stronger the neural connections, the quicker the brain responds.

Pairing brain training with school readiness is a natural way to make a difficult task fun & easier. Learning difficulties can often be a result of left brain weakness. Using brain training exercises strengthens both hemispheres while improving working memory, sequencing and brain processing speed.

The results are often remarkable. Students learn the material quicker and easier. They are better able to retain the information and have faster recall, resulting in higher academic achievement, better test scores and school success.

The brain training grids are laid out in a systematic order. Your student should move through the book from beginning to end.

Brain Training grids start at the top left corner and move right across the row. We then move to the row below the one completed and move left to right, continue in this fashion, ending with the bottom right square of the grid. In the following example, the squares are numbered for you.

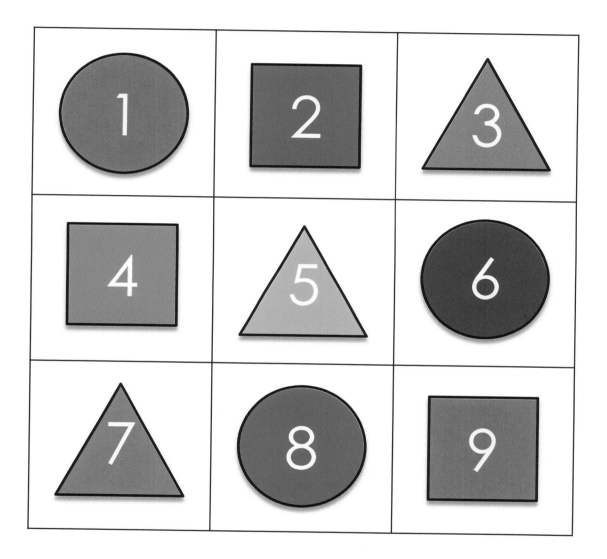

The grids are arranged systematically from simple to more complex, therefore they should be completed in order. Each grid should be done multiple times to assure mastery before moving to the next grid.

Name the Color. Start at the top left square of the grid and name the colors. Record your time and try to beat it!

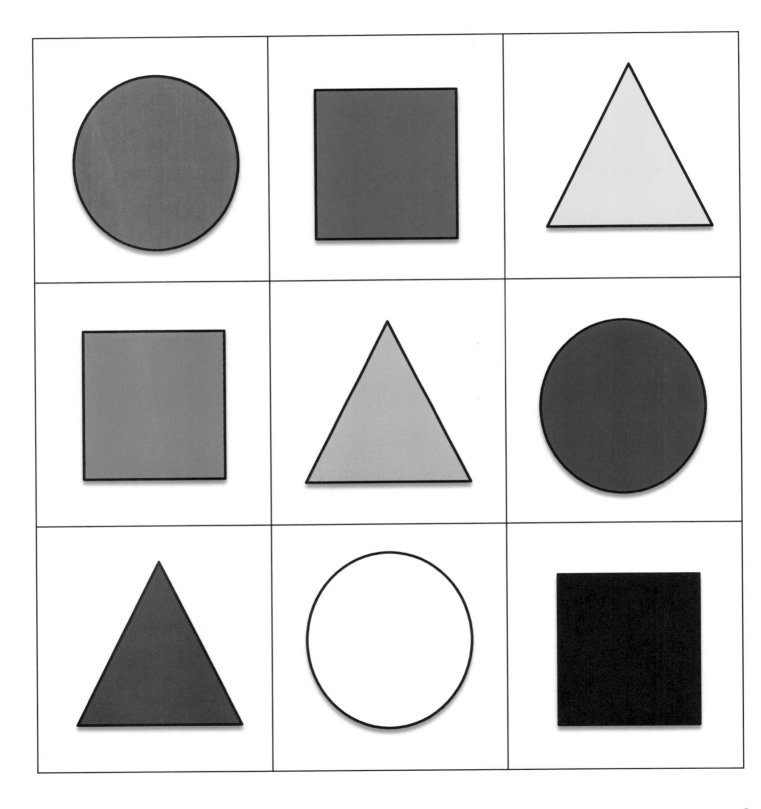

Name the Color and Shape. Start at the top left square of the grid and name the color first and then the shape.
i.e. "red circle, blue square, yellow triangle..." Record your time and try to beat it!

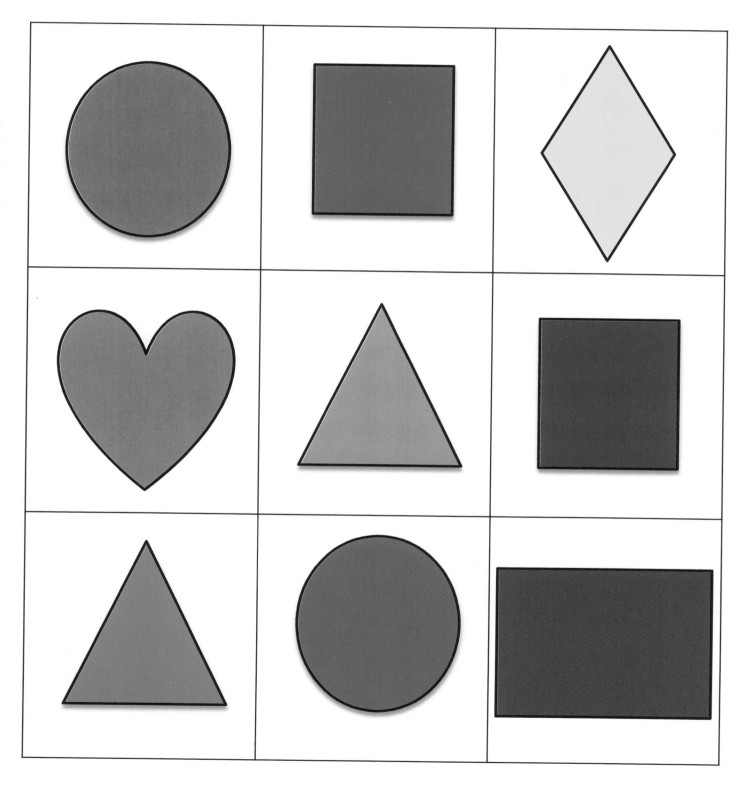

Read the Color Word. Start at the top left square of the grid and read the color words. Record your time and try to beat it!

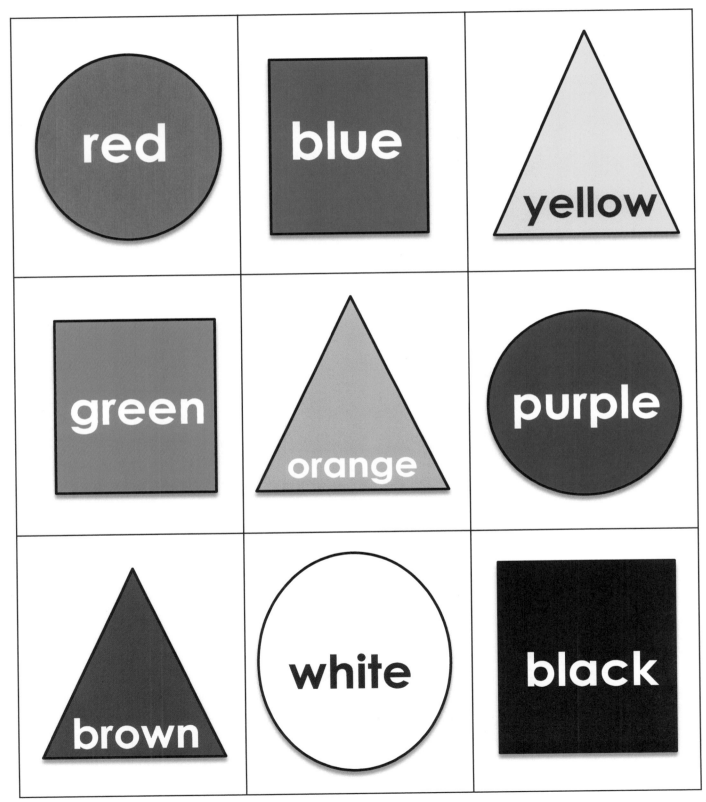

1. **Read the Color Word:** Read each color word.

black   purple   

orange   brown   red

green   yellow   blue

1. **Read the Color Word:** Read each color word.

black   purple   white

orange   brown   red

green   yellow   blue

1. **Read the Color Word:** Read each color word.

2. **Read the Color Word and Name the Color of the word:**
   Now say the color first and then read the shape word. i.e.
   "blue red, green black, red purple…"

red	black	purple
orange	white	blue
yellow	brown	green
green	brown	yellow
blue	black	orange
purple	white	red

Brain Training
SHAPES

Bridgette Sharp

heart

square

triangle

square   diamond circle

triangle   heart   rectangle

circle

square

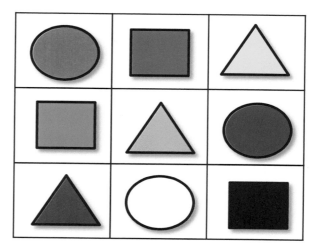

Name the Shape. Start at the top left square of the grid and name the shapes. Record your time and try to beat it!

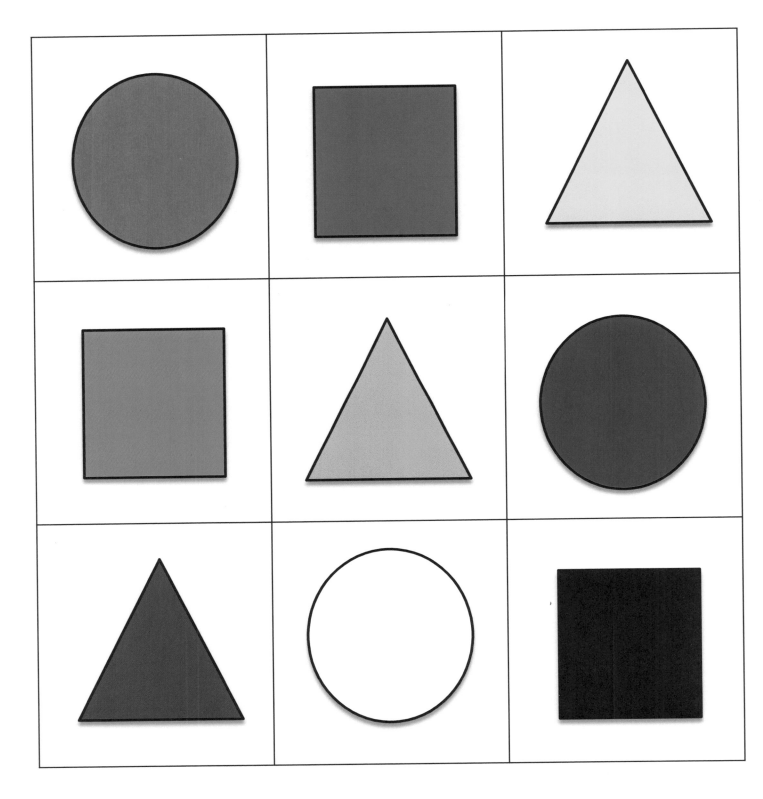

Name the Color and Shape. Start at the top left square of the grid and name the color first and then the shape.
i.e. "red circle, blue square, orange triangle..." Record your time and try to beat it!

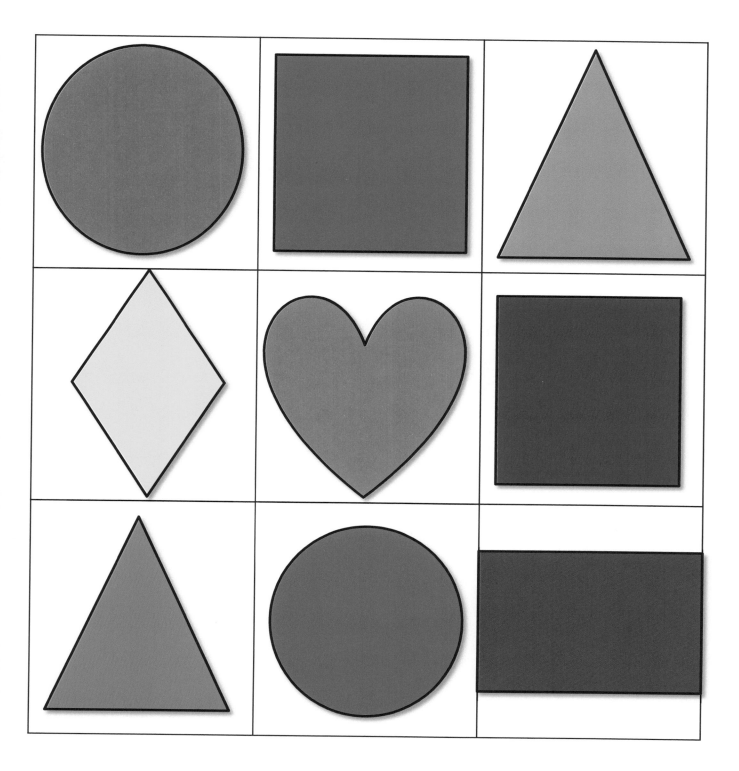

1. **Name the Shape**: Name each shape.

2. **Read the Color and the Shape**: Now say the color first and then the shape. i.e. "purple circle, green square…"

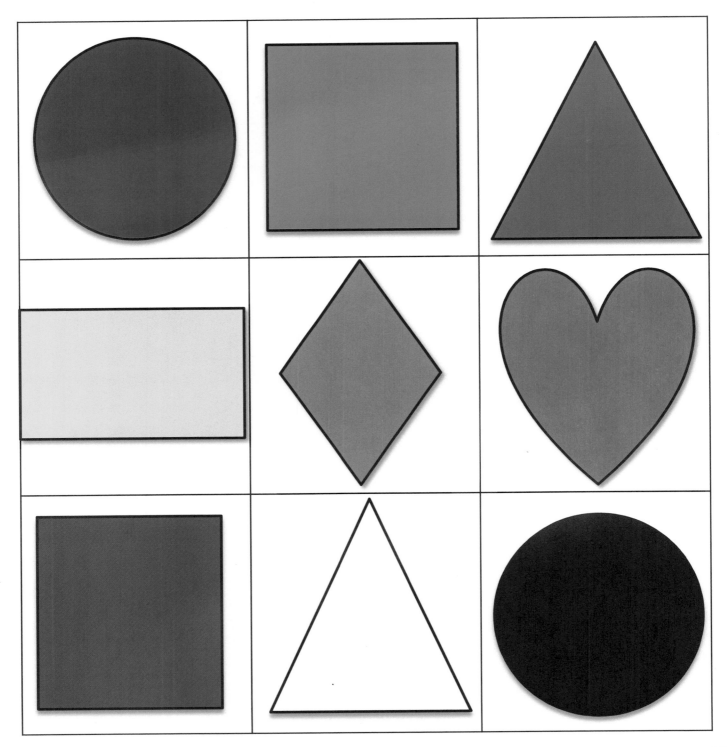

1. **Read the Shape Word:** Read each shape word.

2. **Name the Color and Read the Word**: Now say the color first and then read the shape word. i.e. "red square, green circle…"

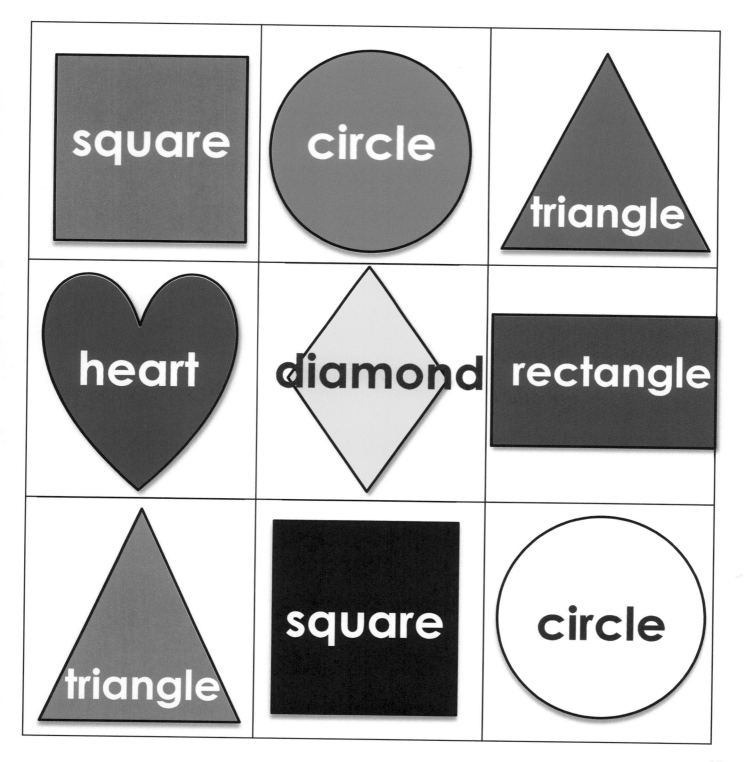

1. **Read the Shape Word:** Read each shape word.

2. **Name the Color and Read the Word:** Now say the color first and then read the shape word. i.e. "orange square, blue circle..."

square   diamond   circle

triangle   heart   rectangle

circle   square   triangle

rectangle   diamond

heart   circle   square

Brain Training

NUMBERS

six	nine	ten
four	eight	five
ten	two	three
five	one	seven
twenty	eleven	seven
one	twelve	two

1. **Read the Number:** Read each number in the shape.

2. **Name the Color and the Number:** Now say the color first and then the number. i.e. "red 9, blue 2..."

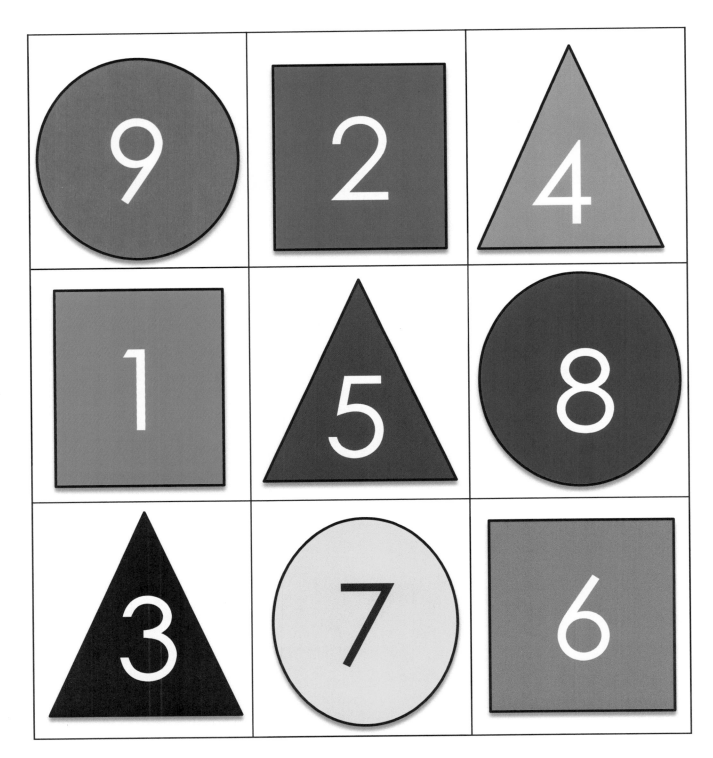

1. **Read the Number:** Read each number in the shape.

2. **Name the Color and the Number:** Now say the color first and then the number. i.e. "pink 11, purple 20..."

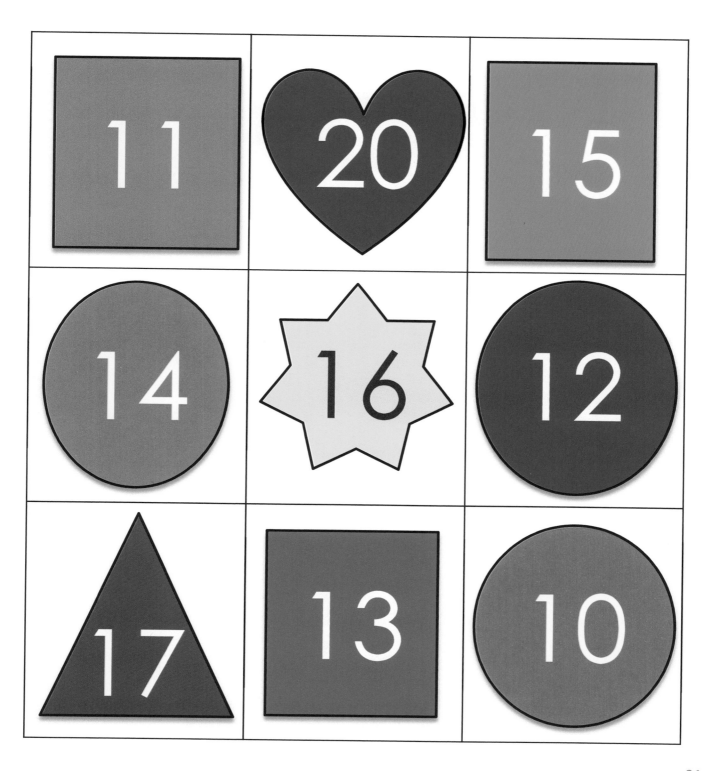

1. **Read the Number:** Read each number in the shape.

2. **Name the Color and the Number:** Now say the color first and then the number. i.e. "yellow 18, pink 20..."

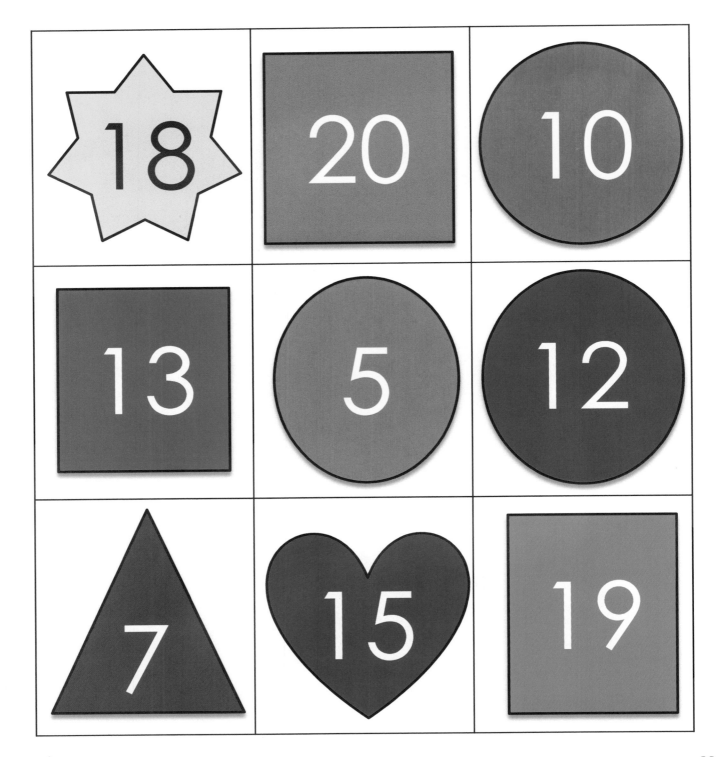

1. **Name the NEXT number:** Name the number that follows the number in the shape. i.e. If you see '9,' say "10."

2. **Name the PREVIOUS Number:** Name the number that comes BEFORE the number in the shape. If you see '9,' say "8." You can refer to a number chart if needed.

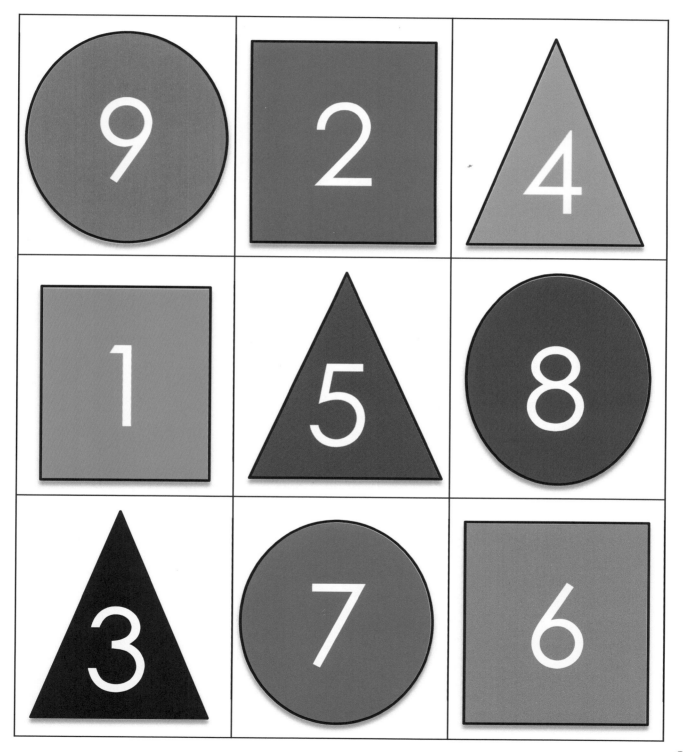

1. **Name the NEXT number:** Name the number that follows the number in the shape. i.e. If you see '10,' say "9."

2. **Name the PREVIOUS Number:** Name the number that comes BEFORE the number in the shape. If you see '10,' say "11." You can refer to a number chart if needed.

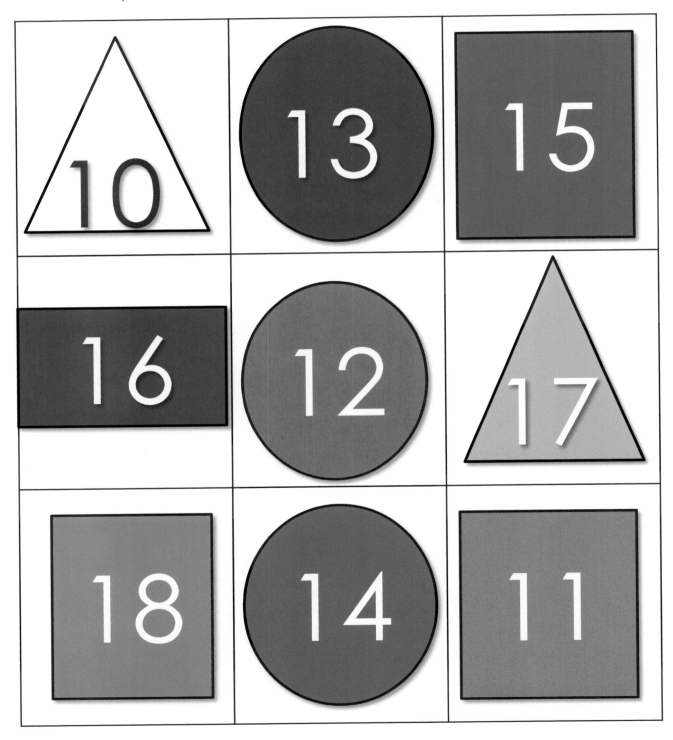

1. **Read the Number Words:** Look at the number in the square and then read the number word.

2. **Name the Color and Read the Word:** Now name the color of the square first and then read the color word. i.e. "yellow one, orange four, red seven…"

1. **Read the Number Words:** Read the number words.

2. **Name the Color and Read the Word:** Now name the color of the square first and then read the word.
i.e. "yellow three, gray four, green five..."

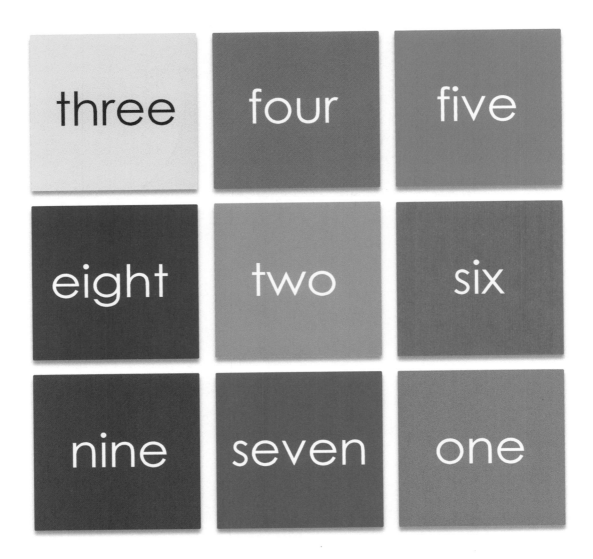

1. **Read the Number Words:** Read the number words.

2. **Name the Color and Read the Word:** Now name the color of the square first and then read the word.
    i.e. "red one, black ten, green two…"

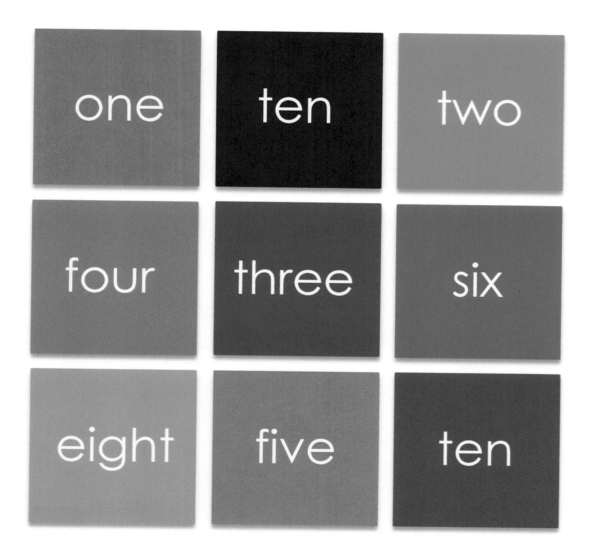

1. **Read the Number Words:** Read the number words.

2. **Read the Word and Name the Color of the Word**: Now read the word and name the color of the word. i.e. " six pink, nine yellow, two green…"

six	nine	ten
four	eight	five
ten	two	three
five	one	seven
twenty	eleven	seven
one	twelve	two

Brain Training
Lower Case
letters

Bridgette Sharp

b		d		f
s	l	e	f	v	d
m	r	b	o	w	n

1. **Name the Lower Case Letters:** Name the letters.

2. **Name the Color of the shape and Name the Letter:** Name the color of the shape and then name the letter in the shape. i.e. "Purple P, Pink C, Gray B..."

1. **Name the Lower Case Letters:** Name the letters.

2. **Name the Color of the shape and Name the Letter:** Name the color of the shape and then name the letter in the shape. i.e. "Green A, Yellow F, Purple M..."

1. **Name the Lower Case Letters:** Name the letters.

2. **Name the Color of the shape and Name the Letter:** Name the color of the shape and then name the letter in the shape. i.e. "Orange i, Pink R, Brown V..."

1. **Name the Lower Case Letters:** Name the letters.

2. **Name the Color of the Letter and Name the Letter:** Name the color of the letter and then name the letter. i.e. "Orange a, Purple L, Red u…"

a	l	u	e	b	d
k	b	m	v	i	l
t	j	c	n	w	o
a	s	i	d	o	x
b	z	r	h	e	p
d	u	y	q	g	f

1. **Name the NEXT Letter:** Do not name the actual letter,, but name the letter in the alphabet that follows it. ie. When you see 'E' , say "F." It may help to have an alphabet chart where your student can refer to it until they know the answers.

e	o	w	p	g	f
b	v	o	h	e	l
u	n	i	d	q	x
m	j	c	r	y	i
k	b	s	z	e	p
a	l	t	a	U	f

1. **Name the PREVIOUS Letter:** Do not name the actual letter,, but name the letter in the alphabet that comes **before** it. ie. When you see 'G' , say "F." It may help to have an alphabet chart where your student can refer to it until they know the answers.

g	a	s	d	f	q
k	j	b	r	z	l
t	l	i	c	q	y
a	u	m	h	d	p
b	U	v	n	g	e
c	e	w	o	f	x

Brain Training
CAPITAL
LETTERS

Bridgette Sharp

G	P	S
S	L	E	F	V	I
A	Z	B	I	F	S

1. **Name the Capital Letters:** Name the letters.

2. **Name the Color of the shape and Name the Letter:** Name the color of the shape and then name the capital letter in the shape. i.e. "Purple P, Pink C, Green B..."

Record your times here!

Date	Time		Date	Time		Date	Time

1. **Name the Capital Letters:** Name the letters.

2. **Name the Color of the shape and Name the Letter:** Name the color of the shape and then name the capital letter in the shape. i.e. "Green A, Yellow F, Purple M..."

Record your times here!

Date	Time		Date	Time		Date	Time

1. **Name the Capital Letters:** Name the letters.

2. **Name the Color of the shape and Name the Letter:** Name the color of the shape and then name the capital letter in the shape. i.e. "Orange i, Pink R, Brown V…"

1. **Name the Capital Letters:** Name the letters.

2. **Name the Color of the Letter and Name the Letter:** Name the color of the letter and then name the capital letter. i.e. "Orange G, Purple A, Red C..."

G	A	C	J	N	Q
S	L	E	F	V	I
A	Z	B	I	F	S
W	G	O	R	E	C
O	U	H	M	R	T
P	K	D	Y	U	B

1. **Name the NEXT Letter:** Do not name the actual letter,, but name the letter in the alphabet that follows it. ie. When you see 'G' , say "H." It may help to have an alphabet chart where your student can refer to it until they know the answers.

G	A	C	J	N	Q
S	L	E	F	V	I
A	Z	B	I	F	S
W	G	O	R	E	C
O	U	H	M	R	T
P	K	D	Y	U	B

1. **Name the PREVIOUS Letter:** Do not name the actual letter,, but name the letter in the alphabet that comes **before** it. ie. When you see 'G' , say "F." It may help to have an alphabet chart where your student can refer to it until they know the answers.

G	A	C	J	N	Q
S	L	E	F	V	I
A	Z	B	I	F	S
W	G	O	R	E	C
O	U	H	M	R	T
P	K	D	Y	U	B

Brain Training
Letter Sounds

Name the Sound. Start at the top left square of the grid and name the sound of the letter in the shape (not the letter).
i.e. " /aaaaa/, /fffff/, /mmmmm/…"
/a/ as in <u>a</u>m, /f/ as in <u>f</u>ish, /m/ as in <u>m</u>ad, /s/ as in <u>s</u>ad,
/n/ as in <u>n</u>o, /l/ as in <u>l</u>ove, /o/ as in <u>O</u>z, /h/ as in <u>h</u>i,
/r/ as in <u>r</u>ed

Name the Color, Letter Name and Sound. Start at the top left square of the grid and name the color first and then name the letter and it's sound.
i.e. "green A /aaa/, blue F /ffff/, purple M /mmmm/..."

Name the Sound. Start at the top left square of the grid and name the sound of the letter in the shape (not the letter). i.e. " /p/, /y/,/c/..."

/p/ as in pie, /y/ as in yak, /c/ as is cat, /b/ as in bat, /g/ as in go, /q/ as in quit, /e/ as in egg, /s/ as in sis, /t/ as in too

Name the Color, Letter Name and Sound. Start at the top left square of the grid and name the color first and then name the letter and it's sound.
i.e. "Purple P /p/, Pink Y /y/, Green C /c/..."

Name the Sound. Start at the top left square of the grid and name the sound of the letter in the shape (not the letter). i.e. "/iiiiiii/, /zzzzzzz/, '/j/..."

/i/ as in igloo, /z/ as in zoo, /j/ as in jet, /k/ as in yak, /u/ as in up, /x/ as in ox, /v/ as in van, /d/ as in dog

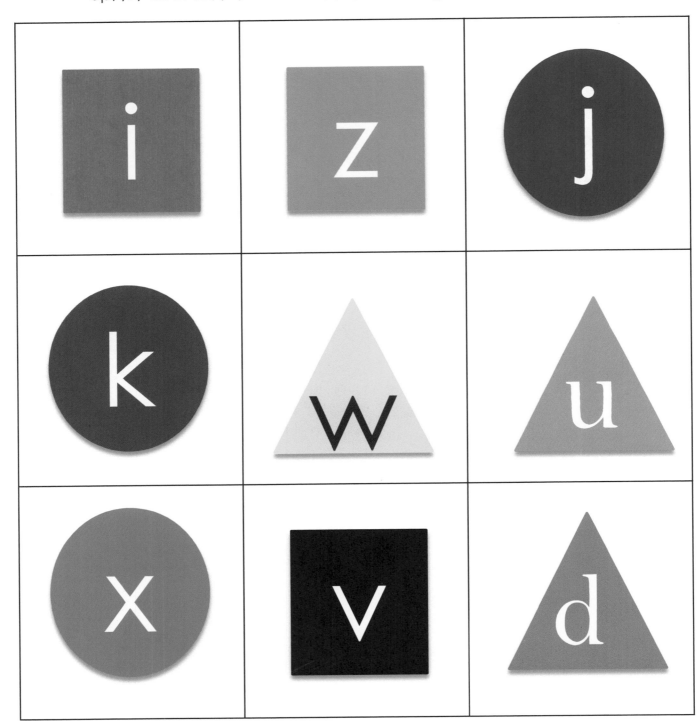

Name the Color, Letter Name and Sound. Start at the top left square of the grid and name the color first and then name the letter and it's sound.
i.e." Red I, /iiii/, Orange Z /zzzz/, Purple J /j/..."

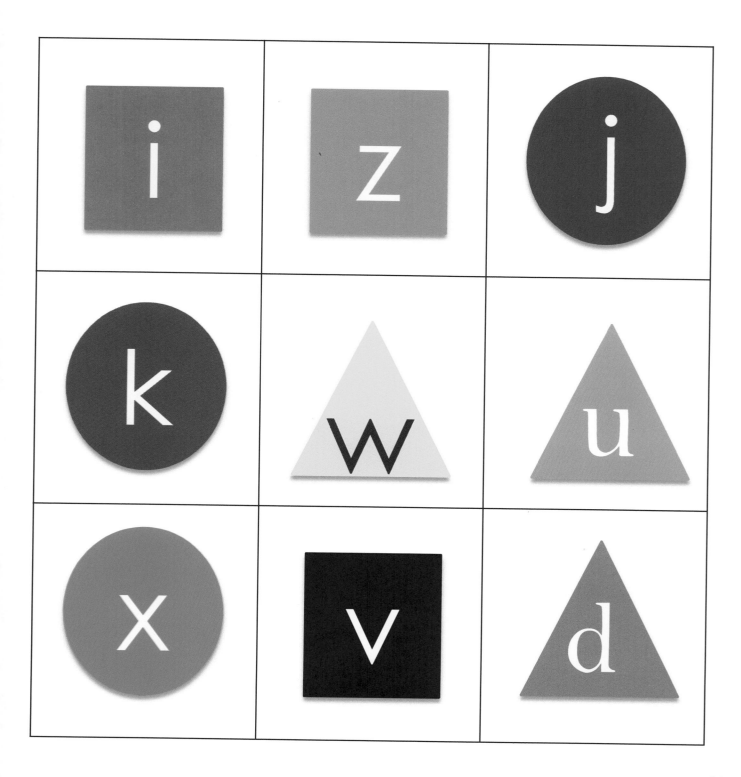

Phonemic Awareness:

1. Read each word to the student and ask "What sound do you hear at the beginning on the word?"

2. Read each word and ask "What sound do you hear at the end of the word?

Brain Training
CVC Words

Bridgette Sharp

Read the CVC Words:

1. "Say it slow." Be careful to blend the sounds together.
2. "Say it fast." Then say the word quickly.
    i.e. "caaaaat, cat, beeeed, bed…"

1. **Read the Words:. Nonsense Words:** "Say it slow." and "Say it fast."

2. **Name the Color and Read the Words:** Name the color first and then read the word quickly. i.e. "blue nun..."

1. **Read the Words:. Nonsense Words:** "Say it slow." and "Say it fast."

2. **Name the Color and Read the Words:** Name the color first and then read the word quickly. i.e. "green gas..."

1. **Read the Words:. Nonsense Words:** "Say it slow." and "Say it fast."

2. **Name the Color and Read the Words:** Name the color first and then read the word quickly. i.e. "blue pez..."

1. **Read the Words:.** "Say it slow." and "Say it fast."

2. **Name the Color and Read the Words:** Name the color first and then read the word quickly. i.e. "red lac…"

1. **Read the Words:.** "Say it slow." and "Say it fast."

2. **Name the Color and Read the Words:** Name the color first and then read the word quickly. i.e. "blue meb..."

1. **Read the Words:.** "Say it slow." and "Say it fast."

2. **Name the Color and Read the Words:** Name the color first and then read the word quickly. i.e. "pink wom…"

1. **Read the Words:.** "Say it slow." and "Say it fast."

2. **Name the Color and Read the Words:** Name the color first and then read the word quickly. i.e. "blue dav..."

OTHER BOOKS BY BRIDGETTE SHARP

Brain Training for Reversals: b-d-p-q

Brain Training for Reversals: t-f-u-n-m-w

Brain Training for Reversals: Numbers & Directions

Brain Training COLORS- Kindle

Brain Training SHAPES –Kindle

Brain Training NUMBERS—Kindle

Brain Training PHONICS -

Kindle

12 Weeks to Superior Memory – Kindle

Neuromotor Brain

Training Exercises – Kindle

Cognitive Training Exercises – Kindle

Brain Balancing Hemispheric Integration

- Kindle

Brain Training ABC's & 123's: Kindergarten Readiness – Kindle

Brain Training Capital Letters – Kindle

Brain Training Sight Words: 100 HF

Words –Kindle

Brain Training Letter Sounds – Kindle

Brain Training CVC Words – Kindle

Brain Training Lower Case Letters - Kindle

Hacking Consciousness: Life's Little Cheat Codes - Kindle

Brain Training Exercises to Boost Brain Power: for Improved Memory, Focus & Cognitive Function-
Kindle

12 Weeks to Superior Memory & Mental Clarity: The Ultimate Cognitive Enhancement Program

Brain Training ABC's & 123's: Kindergarten Readiness Workbook

Brain Training Boot Camp: Be Sharper, Faster, Smarter

Brain Training Exercises to Boost Brain Power: for Improved Memory, Focus & Cognitive Function

Brain Training First Grade Sight Words: First Grade High Frequency Words

Brain Training Phonics: A Whole Brain Approach to Learning Phonics

Brain Training Second Grade Sight Words

Brain Training Sight Words: 1000 High Frequency Words Every Student Must Know

Brain Training Sight Words Grades 1 -3

Brain Training Sight Words Grades 4 - 6

OTHER BOOKS BY BRIDGETTE SHARP

Brain Training Sight Words Upper Levels

Brain Training Third Grade Sight Words

Creative Exercises for Boosting Brain Power: Creatively Boost Memory, Focus, Attention and Brain Balancing

Hacking Consciousness: Life's Little Cheat Codes

Hands On Phonemic Awareness Workbook

Hands On Reading Drills Workbook

Raise Reading Scores in 5 Minutes a Day

Reading Drills Kids Need to be Fast Readers: Raise Reading Test Scores

Sight Word Phonics: Learn Phonics with High Frequency Words

Sight Word Spinners 1000: Simple & Fun Practice for 1000 High Frequency Words

Sight Word Spinners Grades 1 – 3: Simple & Fun Practice for 300 High Frequency Words

Soul Lessons Adult Coloring Book

Spirit Animals Adult Coloring Book

ONE LAST THING

If you enjoyed this book or found it useful I'd be very grateful if you'd post a short review on Amazon. Your support really does make a difference. I read all of the reviews personally and use the information to produce future publications.

CPSIA information can be obtained at www.ICGtesting.com
Printed in the USA
BVIW12n0121310817
493625BV00012B/38